Crayonimals

"Take a Chalk on the Wild Side"

A coloring book for the kid in all of us!

Crayonimals are hand drawn original designs. Therefore you may see pencil marks or imperfections as can only be found in illustrations drawn by hand.

Crayonimals are NOT computer generated! They are original drawings by a real artist and inspired by a love for, yes, crayons, and animals.

When coloring illustrations in Crayonimals, you are supporting the arts!

Author, artist, bad karaoke singer Nancy J. Bailey is the mom of a horse named Clifford who paints with watercolor. The only horse in the world who signs his own biography, Clifford of Drummond Island visits schools and libraries and assisted living centers, making the world a better place.

Other Books By Nancy J. Bailey

Clifford of Drummond Island

Return to Manitou

Clifford's Bay

The North Side of Down (2015 B.R.A.G. Medallion winner)

My Best Cat

Holding the Ladder

The Sleeping Lion

Eagle Flier

25 Ways To Raise a Great Puppy

15 Rules for Clicker Training Your Horse

15 Rules for Clicker Training Your Dog

15 Rules for Clicker Training Your Cat

www.ingramcontent.com/pod-product-compliance
Lightning Source LLC
Chambersburg PA
CBHW081132280526
45787CB00007B/3053